CONTENTS

Dedication v
Preface vii

Chapter One 1
   In the Beginning
   Dating Outside Your Ethnicity

Chapter Two 13
   Are You Serious!
   Will You Marry Me

Chapter Three 25
   God-Ordained
   What God Has Joined Together;
     Let No Man Put Asunder

Chapter Four 33
   Get In Where You Fit In
   Friends or Not

Chapter Five 47
   Mixed Up!
   Children

Chapter Six 57
    Happily Ever After
    Forever I Do

Chapter 7 69
    Last Words
    The Church

References 81

IT'S NOT BLACK, IT'S NOT WHITE

Being In An Inter-~~Racial~~ Ethnic Marriage

RON AND FELICIA PORTWINE

Copyright © 2022 Ronald and Felicia Portwine

ALL RIGHTS RESERVED.

This book contains material protected under International and Federal Copyright Laws and Treaties. Any unauthorized reprint or use of this material is prohibited. No part of this book may be reproduced or transmitted in any form or by any means, electronic or mechanical, including photocopying, recording, or by any information storage and retrieval system without express written permission from the author/publisher.

Scripture is taken from the New King James Version®. Copyright © 1982 by Thomas Nelson. All rights reserved.

Book Cover Design: Prize Publishing House

Printed by: Prize Publishing House, LLC in the United States of America.

First printing edition 2022.
Prize Publishing House
P.O. Box 9856, Chesapeake, VA 23321
www.PrizePublishingHouse.com

ISBN (Paperback): 978-1-7379751-7-5
ISBN (E-Book): 978-1-7379751-8-2

Library of Congress Control Number: 2022903339

DEDICATION

Ron and I would like to thank our two beautiful and talented daughters. You are a blessing sent from God. And to our granddaughter, Grandy and Grammy (Ma Ma) will always love you! To our families that have supported this union from the beginning without hesitation, we love you and thank you from the bottom of our hearts. To our friends that have stuck by us through the years, we say God bless you and thank you for being a part of this journey.

PREFACE

In this book, Ron and I would like to introduce a woman and a man who have been married outside their ethnicity for over thirty-five-plus years. The joining of two to become one; God-ordained. We had to be able to let go of the stereotypical thinking that God only ordained Black for Black and White for White or whatever the ethnic case may be. However, Felicia will be honest enough to say, of course, that growing up, this topic was never a verbal conversation but an unspoken rule in her home. Listen, this was definitely not something she had in mind when thinking about being married. As a matter of fact, when Ron asked her to marry him, her response was, "**Are You Serious?**" On the other hand, Ronald was already exposed to the interethnic culture. Actually, it was the norm for him! And according to him, this would be his destiny. So we pray that after reading *It's Not Black; And It's Not White*, you will allow your minds and your hearts to be open to the fact that only God determines who is set aside and set apart for each other. Not society! Have you ever just thought about it from that point of view? If not, then read **our** story of how we have traveled through this daunting journey together, knowing God alone designed and predestined us for each other. It hasn't been easy, but definitely doable.

CHAPTER ONE

IN THE BEGINNING
DATING OUTSIDE YOUR ETHNICITY

FELICIA

Dating outside your ethnicity - wow, who would have thought it, this little Black girl from a small town in Arkansas *(yes, ARKANSAS)* would grow up to marry outside her ethnicity. Definitely not her! Well, this brings her and her soulmate to writing this book to hopefully help the world **look** beyond what you **see** and begin to have an open mind that God alone ordains marriage. I know to some that sounds crazy, but for others, well!!!! Follow the journey. It's been over thirty-five-plus years, and I haven't looked back. Trust me; this is not what I dreamed of growing up. This wasn't my tall **dark,** and handsome that I had heard about all my life. Quite the contrary! Let me back up. I got the tall and handsome right, just not the dark.

This relationship started with me needing a place to stay (for a while). However, I've never left. One month led to two months, and three months led to four months, and within six months, we were married. Yep married! I was twenty, and he was twenty-one. Looking back, I can't say I would recommend that simply because we were just kids. We shudder at the thought of our girls marrying at that age. We had a lot of learning and growing up to do. Although they were rough beginnings, we have grown together through the years, laughed together, and often cried together. Most importantly, we have loved together. We met when Ron was thirteen and I was twelve. We would see each other from time to time, but this wasn't someone I was going to marry. Frankly, I didn't even like him, and oh yeah, he was White. Of course, you know how the story ends (the book). Okay, let's get back on track.

I had graduated high school and moved to attend college. I attended about one and a half years before deciding I wanted/needed to work full time. I lived on my own in a little apartment located in an alley. Literally! One night as I lay in bed, I heard this noise outside my window. As I looked out the window, I saw my car being pushed down the alley. I quickly ran outside, screaming, "Please don't take my car!" Well, they didn't, and I was afraid to live alone in that apartment after that incident. After about a couple of days, I remember lying in bed one night and praying to God regarding my next move. I mean, there was no way I could continue to live there. One of the things I said was, "God, I'm ready to be a wife." This was somewhat of a shock, and I was like, where did that come from? Of all the things to be praying about, this was my prayer. A few weeks had gone by, and I decided to reach out to a family member to see if I could come and live with them for a while. Little did I know this would be the beginning of what is now over thirty-five-plus years of marriage. Remember me saying my husband and I had met when I was twelve and he was thirteen? Well, he was a part of the family member's family. Don't ask questions; just read the book, lol. So, to my amazement, he was the one sent to help move me.

When I saw him, I thought to myself, of all people, **HIM**! This really can't be happening. Surely not him. Having no other choice but to let him move me, we began to talk about where I would be staying, and at that moment, he looked at me and said, "You can room with me." Seriously! What, no way! I don't even like you, I thought to myself. I hurried and tried to change the subject, but somehow we kept ending up there. He owned a two-bedroom mobile home (trailer) and suggested that I rent the second bedroom for $75 a month. Hmm, I thought to myself, this just might work. It didn't matter at that moment that I didn't like him. So, I agreed. You have to read my book *You Knew Me*

Then, but You See Me Now to understand these next few statements. So, I moved in. Shortly afterward, we started dating. A couple of weeks went by, and I knew I had to tell my mother I was living with Ron. What a shock to her, to say the least. It had only been a short time since I had left home, and despite all the stuff that had recently come to light, this was just another disappointment, and of course, it didn't help the fact that he was White. I understood her response concerning him being White. Because, again, this was never something we discussed, but certainly an unspoken rule. Marrying outside your ethnicity is taboo and frowned upon by many ethnicities. I am sure this is the case in many households around the world.

RONALD

It was Christmas 1977 when I first met Felicia. She was twelve, and I was thirteen. I remember vividly seeing her for the first time and thinking she was beautiful; something about her made me pause, and I knew then that I was going to marry her. This was God instilling in me the desire to make her my wife. I knew from that first meeting she was meant for me. Yes, I was thirteen and knew without a doubt. No explanation for it; it was just in me. God had put in motion the future of a great and successful marriage that would stand the test of time. Dreaming about her often and seeing us together as an elderly couple would be consistent. (I still dream about her today). She would often consume my thoughts, and I was unsure what to do. Every so often, I would see her, and the inner witness kept getting stronger. Typically it was always around the holidays. Not knowing how to act around her and often being standoffish, I just didn't know how to be near her with all the feelings and emotions I had concerning her.

Looking back on when she moved to Little Rock for college, I was thinking, "How can I get close to her?" At this time, I was nineteen and had a mobile home on an acre of land. This land was next to her family member, and she would visit from time to time. When I found out she would be visiting, I made sure to be there to see her, even if it was from a distance. Time went by, and I kept having the same reaction every time I would get near her or see her. Knowing even more, from within, she was who I would marry and spend my life with. My problem was I didn't know how to act or even speak to her without being, as she says, "rude." Then the opportunity came.

This opportunity was her needing a place to stay because of how unsafe she felt in her apartment after someone tried to steal her car. I remember being part of a conversation concerning this event, seeing this as an opening to get close to her and hopefully spend some time with her to verify what I already knew. Making her an offer to rent my extra room for $75 monthly seemed reasonable, so this was my way in. That was the best decision I ever made. She accepted! Wow, she actually accepted! It was the end of October 1985 when I helped her move in. In my mind, this was my chance to get close to her and realize if these feelings were real or just in my head. By this time, I was twenty-one, and she was just about to turn twenty.

After getting her moved in, I started talking with her about everything and nothing. It just felt right, and it was easy talking to her like she was my best friend. Making sure we spent time together. I found ways to make it happen. We went out a few times for dinner and movies. She saw this as free meals and free entertainment; I saw it as a way to get closer to her. Then during that Christmas, 1985, she went back home for a few days, and I was alone with my thoughts. I went to a family Christmas party and really wasn't there, mentally. Overcome with thoughts about her and what was deep inside urging me, ask her to marry you. I left the family party and went to some friends' party and really wasn't there either. Just in body, not in mind. Being consumed with my feelings about her and what I should do next was at the forefront. I was besieged, consumed, and overwhelmed with thoughts of her!

I was trying desperately not to think about this Felicia. I was remembering all the dreams as they flooded back through my mind. The thoughts were overwhelmingly painful to the degree that relief was needed. My stomach was in knots; the thought of marriage ran through my mind so much I directed a conversation with my friends at the party, telling them how much Felicia meant to me and the desire to marry her was overpowering. Their response was, "Okay, then do it." They liked Felicia and thought we made a good couple. How would she react, and what would she say?

She was twenty, and I twenty-one. I believed we were old enough to get married. However, looking back, we were just kids. But this was a move in the right direction. I had a pretty good job, a home, I loved her, and I wanted to be with her. What else is there? What God foreordains will come to pass, regardless of the paths you take. He will make it happen.

Knowing now, after thirty-five-plus years, God was in the mix. He was urging me with every turn that I was to marry Felicia and devote my life to her. Wow! God was even working thru my friends. Looking back, it all becomes clear and precise, down to the very millisecond of my actions. Felicia was to be my bride. I have never doubted this fact and am so thankful for doing what God directed. If I had missed what God had for me, I would not be who I am today!

CHAPTER TWO

ARE YOU SERIOUS! WILL YOU MARRY ME

FELICIA

Will you marry me? Seventy-five dollars was a lot of money over thirty-five years ago. Well, just to let you know, he still hasn't received the seventy-five dollars. Reluctantly I agreed, and we made the arrangement for me to rent the room. That was the agreement, or so I thought. Of course, it wasn't long before we would begin hanging out and talking more. I was still doing my thing, working and dating; I mean, we were just roommates. Finally, one day he asked me out to dinner. I thought free meal. And so I said yes, that sounded like it would be nice. Never thinking he had an ulterior motive. One date led to two dates and then three, and so on. You are getting the picture, right?

After about a month of getting free food, I began to look at him a little differently. He was not so bad after all. Still not thinking anything of it, I began to have these feelings; it was like I just wanted to be with him. However, my mind was saying NO, you know this will not work for many reasons. I soon dismissed those thoughts and decided to give it a try. We had a lot of fun together. We did things I had never seen, imagined, or experienced, like going to the movies, eating at different restaurants, traveling, and just enjoying each other's company. One night when I came home from work, he was sitting in the living room playing music. He knew I loved music and loved to dance. The lights were dim as if he was trying to set the mood. I/we started to dance, and to my amazement, he reached in for a kiss. I felt kind of awkward at first; I mean, I had never kissed someone outside my ethnicity before. It felt a little strange at first. As the night went on, we continued playing music and dancing. We parted to our separate rooms for the night. As I lay in bed thinking about what had happened, there was this feeling of he's not so bad, and my mind/heart said, "I kind of like him." Soon dismissing the thought, I fell asleep.

The next morning, he had already gone to work, and I also had to get ready for work. That evening after work, we both were sitting and talking, and out came these words, "Would you consider dating a White man?" Well, as I stumbled through my words, "I've never thought about it." I replied. Ron prides himself on being a smooth talker, lol. So the story begins. After we started dating, things began to move fast. Let me pause to say that my parents were not happy about the idea of me dating someone White, but I had been living on my own for some time and didn't feel as though I was being disrespectful or out of line. This was not something that I had set out to do. This just happened; I mean, I didn't set out looking for this. Knowing what I know now, this was the plan of God and God-ordained. As I stated, things were moving pretty fast. One night as I was cooking dinner (chicken), he was watching T.V., and I heard him call my name. I looked around the corner, and he was kneeling next to a chair and motioned for me to come and sit down. As I moved slowly to the chair and sat down, he looked me in the eyes and asked, "Will you marry me?" And without hesitation, I said, "**Are you serious?**" Side note he didn't present a ring. LOL!!

RONALD

After spending time with her, I knew she was my destiny. I was not sure how this was going to play out. How do I do this? Ask her to marry me? What am I doing? I was so nervous and thought, we have only been going out a couple of months, and how will she react. I mean she was staying in my home. If she says no, do I let her stay? Do I stop taking her out? Do I remain cordial? What? WHAT WILL SHE SAY? I was petrified. The uncertainties seemed to be crushing me. Doubt was trying to creep in. However, there was an inward assurance that drove me towards her, and I was unable to have any other thoughts except about her.

Focusing on anything else was impossible. Going back to the Christmas party, I left with the thought, "I AM GOING TO DO THIS!" Not sure how. I didn't have much money and could not afford to buy a ring. Nevertheless, I was going to do it and do it quickly. No hesitation, I was sure of this. When she comes back from the Christmas visit to her home, this is when I would ask her. Felicia got back on December 26, 1985. From that day till the asking day is a blur. I only remember working and hanging out with her at some of our friends' house for a couple of nights. I planned to do this ASAP. My heart was racing, and fear was trying to stop me. What God has ordained cannot be un-ordained.

The night came, Thursday, January 2, 1986. The realization of us dating for only a couple of months flooded my mind. Was it too soon? What will her response be? What will happen next? There was an inner tumult happening. However, I knew this was right, and I was going to spend the rest of my life with her as my wife. I mean, I had been dreaming about her since I was thirteen. How could I not be with her? That night is still thriving and alive in my memory. On January 2, 1986, she was in the kitchen frying some chicken wings, and we were watching "The Cosby Show" on T.V. The episode was "Ms. Westlake." Yes, I remember the day, the date, and what was on T.V. We were both home that night because she didn't have to work, and I made it a point to stay in and not go out. Being so nervous and afraid she would say no, I hesitated until the courage was mustered.

I was sitting in the living room, trying to contain the panic. Getting down on one knee then saying, "Felicia, come in here for a minute. I got something I want to talk to you about." She came around the corner, and seeing her made my heart skip, and I knew right then it was RIGHT! 100% RIGHT! She was/is so beautiful, and I wanted to take care of her and grow old with her. She looked at me with a look of, what is he doing? I asked her to sit down, knowing she did not think this was what was going to happen. I am no great romantic; however, she says I'm a smooth talker. Maybe that helped me. I didn't even have a ring to give her; I just knew I had to do this. It was right then, right there, in the living room of the trailer; there was no doubt this was the time.

She sat down, and I essentially said, "We haven't been dating long, but I love you," as if I was trying to justify what I was about to say to her—trying to be the smooth talker. "Will you marry me?" Her reply gave me a great pause. "Are you serious?" I could never have imagined that would be her reply. At first, devastation hit me like a freight train. Pushing past the overwhelming feeling of devastation, I said, "Yes, I'm serious; I want to marry you and spend my life with you." What kind of answer was, "Are you serious?" Talk about feeling crestfallen. After what seemed like hours, she said yes. It was actually less than a minute, but wow, was I on the edge of a crevasse for that minute. Everything was running through my head. "Was this right?" "Was I really supposed to be with her?" "Maybe I was wrong?" "What do I do now?" I was in a state of panic and not sure what to do next. Then I heard the answer I yearned for.

She said YES! Wow, I was ecstatic. I didn't know what was next. I just knew we were getting married. Letting everyone know was the next. Then the plans ensued.

One of the first things for me was telling my mother. During the conversation, I mentioned that I did not have a ring. My mother insisted on giving me a ring she had and told me to trade it in for a nice wedding set at a place called Service Merchandise. This store has since gone out of business. If the store were still around, I would buy another exact set because the rings were stolen. That was such a heartbreak for us. However, it's okay because God blessed me to design a beautiful one-of-a-kind ring set for her and have them made. After the conversation with my mother, the next had to be done.

Before getting married, I insisted on asking her father for her hand in marriage. We took a trip back to her hometown on a Saturday, riding on my motorcycle. Felicia had made sure her mother knew we were coming and made sure her father would be home. During the ride, I was more nervous about asking him for her hand than asking her to marry me. I know I should have asked him before asking her; however, I knew what his response would be and wanted the commitment from her first. This was a very hard day, and doing this was the right thing to do. Being somewhat old-fashioned and believing a man should ask a father for his daughter's hand in marriage was not only right, but it was also respectful, honorable, and a man's responsibility.

We arrived and parked the motorcycle in front of the house. As we went in, I could feel my heart pounding as if it were a drum on the drumline at halftime of a football game. Going into the living room, I sat down and began speaking to her father and letting him know I intended to marry his daughter and take care of her. That conversation lasted all of about five minutes. His immediate reply was "NO," an emphatic "NO," and he did not approve and would not be attending the wedding to give her away either. He made it very clear that Black and White was not a marriage he accepted. I knew beforehand this would be his response. The truth is I almost didn't ask because I knew this. The fact is, a man stands for what is right and backs it up with his word and, more importantly, his actions.

Leaving there, indignation rose within me, I was going to prove him wrong, and that was that! Felicia was crying on the way back. Her hurt was agonizing to me. I wanted to fix it. I wanted to make it better. I wanted him to see she would be happy with me and that we were made for each other. Telling him he was wrong would have given me so much satisfaction. However, that was not what God wanted. After we were married, God made sure that I never disrespected or acted differently toward him. I would always be cordial every time we met. That was hard for me, although it was doable with God's help. Every time I saw him, I would invite him to our home. I did my best to make him know he was welcome and that I had moved past his NO. Some eleven years of marriage went by, me inviting him numerous times every year, and the answer was always NO. My determination outlasted him.

After eleven years of marriage, on Labor Day 1997, while doing some backyard work, the girls came to the door saying granny was here. I thought, okay, my mother is here. I said, "Okay, I will be in when finished." They then proceeded to say, "Granny and Papa are here." I dropped the string trimmer and went immediately into the house. Yep, sure enough, he had finally made his way to our home. What a miracle that was. I gave him the nickel tour of the house and yard. This was the chance to let him see that I was doing what I promised, and that was I would take care of his daughter and give her the best I could. Afterward, he made a statement essentially saying he could see that I was taking care of her and was thankful for me being a man of my word. Since that first visit, he would come to the house at various times for holidays and when he had doctor's visits in town. He would hang out with me, and when we saw people he knew, he would introduce me as his son-in-law. Wow, isn't God awesome! I believe that is one aspect of Proverbs 18:22, "He who finds a wife finds a good thing and obtains **favor** from the Lord" (NKJV). Her father favored me, and that was a miracle!

By the way, I never got that rent money. Still a little livid about that.

CHAPTER THREE

GOD-ORDAINED
WHAT GOD HAS JOINED TOGETHER; LET NO MAN PUT ASUNDER

FELICIA

Mark 10:8-9 states, "And the two shall become one flesh; so then they are no longer two, but one flesh. Therefore what God has joined together, let not man separate" (NKJV). Yes, he was serious! That scripture speaks volumes and sums up the matter. Marriage is ordained by God, not man. Throughout this book, we will be using the word ethnicity and not race. There is only one race, the **human race.** In the beginning, I did consider **our** marriage interracial. However, over time I just saw myself married to Ron, another member of the human race.

Remember when I spoke regarding marrying outside your ethnicity was not a topic of discussion in my home but an unspoken rule? Again this wasn't something I had set out to do or ever thought about; however, when this happened, I had a peace that surpassed all understanding, my understanding! I never regarded this as not being normal or different in a sense. Let me explain. In my mind, or how I saw it, he was a man, and I was a woman. Meaning he was a man, just that, a man. I mean, of course, I knew he was White, and I was definitely not in denial of that. Haven't we all heard the saying, "I don't see color?" For me, that's not a true statement. I saw color: **White!** Yes, I saw a White man. But for some reason, I didn't feel any type of way other than I was falling in love with him despite the color of his skin.

My response to his proposal was not the fact that he was White but merely the thought of what others would say (family, outsiders, and the world) and that someone could actually love me for me. Read my book, *You Knew Me Then, But You See Me Now*. Talk about a feeling I never had before; this was very new and very refreshing, to say the least. After my initial response to the question ("Are you serious?"), of course, I said yes. We actually dated for six months and married. Why so soon? Well, remember the seventy-five dollars for rent that he never received. Read between the lines.

When you know better, you do better. A quote from Maya Angelou, "Do the best you can until you know better. Then, when you know better, do better"(Angelou, M., 2013, June 24). In other words, according to James 4:17 (NKJV), "Therefore, to him (her) who knows to do good and does not do it, to him (her) it is sin." So for Ron and me, we knew better. This is why we titled this chapter God-Ordained. There was something on the inside of us both that said, "We want God to be the head of this marriage." So on April 5, 1986, we stood before God and declared **our** vows to each other, to love, honor, and cherish until death do us part.

RONALD

What the heck was I thinking? I was not prepared for the next, even though I thought I was. We first set a date for Saturday, June 6, 1986. However, a couple of weeks went by, and we knew we had to move the date up. God ordained this relationship; why wait? That is why we knew we had to move the date. I didn't know much about God or the Bible, unlike Felicia. However, we did know that we were not living the way God wanted, and that had to be corrected. We knew we wanted to put God first in **our** marriage. This is why we thoroughly believe we have had a successful marriage for over thirty-five years and counting.

Saturday, April 5, 1986. We said **our** vows and committed to each other, to love, honor, and cherish until death do us part. This sounds good and all but remember, we are a couple with different ethnic backgrounds. She is Black, and I am White. What difference does it make? None as far as I was concerned. I was raised to see people as people no matter the color of their skin. I know what you think. Is that really true? How is that possible when being White and growing up during that time? All because of what society says are you asking these types of questions. Let me explain. My mother had been married to my stepdad, a Black man, for eight years by this time. I had no preconceived ideas of ethnic differences concerning whether people are not supposed to marry outside their ethnicity. My mother raised me to treat everyone equally regardless of their skin color. She always said, "Never judge a person by the color of their skin." She made sure I understood and knew that people were all the same other than how they were raised based on their ethnic family background. Her teaching aligned with God's Word. John 7:24 states, "Do not judge according to appearance but judge with righteous judgment" (NKJV). I'm not sure whether she knew the Bible backed up what she taught me. Although I am very thankful, this is what she instilled in me. I do know this solidified the fact that I only saw Felicia as a woman, a woman I wanted to marry and spend my life with. Irrespective of her being **Black** and me being **White**, we were in the SOUTH and of different ethnic backgrounds. So what!

In the south, during that time, people still frowned on this type of marriage or relationship, as some still do today. We were breaking the stereotypical mindset. It didn't matter, and I was moving forward regardless of what people may have thought or said. It was easy for me to love her. I only saw her as a gift from God. A woman who stole my heart when I was thirteen. Even my friends only saw her as Felicia.

My true friends didn't care; they were happy for me. They only expressed concern because they knew the plight we were about to undertake and how people would react towards us. None of them questioned **our** love. They thought we might be a little crazy; nonetheless, they supported us. There were some so-called friends that made statements like, "You won't make it a year." Then I learned once we made it that first year they said we wouldn't make it five years. Well, thirty-five-plus years later, we are still together. Some of those same so-called friends have been married more than once to someone from the same ethnic background. Huh.

I must input a statement here made by my boss at the time when I showed him Felicia's picture. There were two Ron's in this shop, so the owner, Forrest, called me Reginald. (Just an FYI). Forrest said to me, "Reginald, she's a beautiful young lady. If you love her, then, by all means, marry her. Just know it will be a tough row to hoe living in the south. Otherwise, be strong and stand your ground. I'm happy for you." That statement still resonates with me to this day. I can honestly say we have had some interesting experiences with people concerning this Black and White thing. When will people see past the…? Well, you know.

CHAPTER FOUR

GET IN WHERE YOU FIT IN FRIENDS OR NOT

FELICIA

Are you our friend or not? "When someone shows you who they are, believe them the **first** time." – Maya Angelou (Angelou, M., Goodreads) Unfortunately for Ron and me, some of our friends stayed, and some left, even family. Most of his friends stayed because this was not out of the norm for them. But for me, well, let's just say everyone wasn't happy and remember my dad being one of them. Please don't misunderstand; I do not deny the struggles our forefathers endured or the struggles that we as a people continue to endure. No, quite the opposite. I think there is a misconception regarding couples who date or marry outside their ethnicity. For me, this was never something I was dreaming of or even thinking about regarding being married. It's not that we (I) turned a blind eye or deny that racism exists; it is very real and present even in 2022. However, I didn't go looking for this, but it came looking for me, God-ordained.

For me, the decision to go outside one's ethnicity was to step back and try and look at the big picture and do a lot of soul searching. I mean, was I really ready for this, was I even mature enough to understand what I was about to embark upon, and was I ready for the feedback of my parents, friends, and not to mention the thought of what society as a whole would say or how they viewed such a union. One has to be mature and ready to take on all that comes with the choice to engage in what society sees as taboo. But at that very moment of saying yes, I knew I was up for whatever my future held for me as long as I had Ron by my side. As a matter of fact, we/couples who dare to go outside their ethnicity usually get double the racism. In the Black community, you are seen as selling out, and in the White community, you are looked upon as to say, how dare you! Of course, for Ron, the Black community still looks at him as a racist, and the White community looks at him as an n…. lover. Yep, you read that right. Putting this in black and white (on paper) seems so senseless, disturbing, and so unpleasant. But this is reality.

Yes, we have come a long way as people; however, we still have a long way to go. If we never learn from history, we are sure to keep repeating it. The friends that I lost really weren't a loss. Yes, it hurt at the time, but a friend should be a FRIEND! According to Proverbs 17:17 (NKJV), "A friend loves at all times." Despite the fact that my dad didn't agree or give his blessing, I still chose to marry the man I had fallen in love with. My mother wasn't excited about the idea either, but she chose to accept it (not initially); however, it was sooner than my dad. Thirty-five-plus years later, I don't regret my decision to marry outside my ethnicity. The thing I love most about my husband: I didn't have to change who I was. I didn't have to choose to be Black or try to be White because the fact of the matter is I am BLACK. Ron had no preconceived ideas of how I should be. He loved me for me.

I don't feel like I get a pass with society because my husband is White, oh no, no, no. I can't just go to the front of the line. And believe it or not, Mr. Gas, water, and electric say you must pay your bill on time every time!! LOL. No passes there either. See, we are just like any other married couple. I must admit during the first few years of marriage, when I met someone or started a new job, this was not the first thing people got to know about me. Talk about the self-inflicted pressure I put on myself just to go along with society's idea of marriage. I wanted them to see me for who I was rather than who I was married to. As time went on, I realized that it was somewhat an issue to some, and it was no big deal to others. Even Ron would not discuss his family with co-workers. In one instance, Ron had a job he was fired from because they learned I was Black. It had nothing to do with his performance because he got three one dollar an hour raises in three months. It was devastating to learn people were this cruel and did not consider he had a family to support. He found out one of the co-workers saw us together at a town carnival while working with the church puppet show team for children. A sad reality! When Ron asked them why he was being let go, the owner told him, "We don't want your kind here." What kind? The truth is a funny thing; for me, when White people would find out about Ron being White, they always had to let me know how many Black friends they have, and when the Black people found out, well, they either liked it, or they didn't. No in-between. Yep!!! People tend to get afraid of the unknown or unspoken. One of the most asked questions about **our** relationship is, "How do we discuss the injustices of our society?" Ron losing his job was a serious injustice. My/**our** response has always been right is right and wrong is wrong. Yes, there have been some very heated conversations regarding the injustices in this world; however, we both understood and understand that this would come into play sooner or later as this comes with the decision of being in the relationship. I have had to explain feelings from my point of view as Ron has explained from his point of view, and we find ourselves meeting in the middle. Learning from each other has made us better. Again we are not blind to the injustices of our society. Dr. Martin Luther King Jr. stated, "Injustice anywhere is a threat to justice everywhere." (King Jr., M. L., 2015, April 11). But as the years went by (over thirty-five-plus years later), it is what it is. No apologies. Again this is **our** journey.

RONALD

At first, I questioned this chapter title God gave Felicia because I fit in everywhere. At the very least, I believe I do. Remember, my mother raised me to see everyone equally regardless of skin color. She would tell me, "Do not judge people based on the color of their skin; see them as people." I knew I was White, but that didn't mean I could or would treat anyone differently. Everyone was the same as far as I was concerned based on how my mother raised me. Truthfully, it was hard growing up in an all-Black community in Arkansas. Not understanding prejudice at that time, I believed everyone was like my mother.

Skin color was not an issue! It didn't take me long to learn she was different and made sure I was different. At the age of eleven, the pressure was tremendous, and I often wondered if she was right. However, I stood my ground and never wavered on the fact all people are the same. Being hurt was hard, but I refused to let people's ignorance dictate how I would treat them. Doing my best to treat everyone equally was difficult, especially being the only White boy on the block. Please know this is not because of skin color on my part. As the only White boy in the neighborhood and the only White boy on the bus, I had to look beyond what people said to me, about me, or about my mother and my stepfather. On the bus, I was bullied with derogatory statements that somehow I, an eleven-year-old White boy, was at fault for their situation and status in life. It was me that didn't want them to succeed or have anything. M.E.?!! What did I do? How am I to blame for anyone's position in life?

I was an eleven-year-old kid. Being called a "Cracker" and "Redneck," I often wondered what that meant. Asking my mother about the meaning of those words and the statements being made, she would tell me they are ignorant and have so much to learn. Well, I had to be strong and accept that my mother was right, even under such tremendous pressure as an eleven-year-old. Before moving to that community, the other places we lived were multi-ethnic. I had always played with everyone and did not hear such statements until we moved there. Even at the new school I attended, many of the White children would find out my stepfather was Black, and they too would make derogatory statements about who my mother was married to. Over time I was able to recognize my true friends. I soon began removing and weeding out those who did not have my best interest at heart. They basically only wanted to hurt me and did not care how it could or would affect me. I maintained my mother's acumens no matter what.

I realized something one day on the bus and said to those who were bullying me, "How am I holding you down? I live next door to you, and I'm only eleven years old." It was then they realized Portwine (everyone called me by my last name) was an okay person and started accepting me for me. I had Black and White friends, and I didn't care about any differences. As I got older and in high school, I found that the world was really messed up with this racial crap. I was weeding out friends again.

High school was all new students with various ethnic backgrounds. The school was near an Air Force base, and many of the students were part of a military family. They were more accepting of all ethnicities. However, many still did not agree with my mother's marriage when they found out. Those needed no more effort. They got weeded out quickly. For the most part, most of my friends were good with me. Like Felicia, I dated; however, I dated Black and White girls. There just weren't any connections with any of them. Felicia was always in my heart, placed there by God, and truly the focus of my heart.

I always knew that Felicia was who I was supposed to be with. Because of the fact that all through high school, I would dream about us growing old together and being parents. From the first time I saw her, I dreamt about her from that moment on. Dating was basically a waste of my time. I had to learn tough valuable lessons, so I never tried to fit in anywhere, thus why I stated at the beginning of this chapter concerning its title. Now I just go with the flow.

Once we became a couple and married, "just me" (Ron) is who I was/am. My thought was, "I'm who I am, and I'm not changing for anyone. "If you like me, okay; if you don't like me, okay." I was with Felicia because of being in LOVE with her. If some of our friends had an issue with that, we would just stop the friendship and move on. Our true friends were of different ethnicities, and we didn't seek out one ethnic background over another. We would allow God to put people in our lives, and we knew who our true friends were. There was always proof laid out before us. God was always guiding us in this area.

We had several friends that we lost touch with over time and now know it was part of God's plan for us. Some people come into your life for a reason, and some for a season. I am convinced that if we had remained friends with some of them, our life and marriage would be totally different; not saying good, bad, or indifferent, just different. As God directed, we made many new friends who have stuck with us the whole thirty-five-plus years and will be in our lives another thirty-five-plus years. We never discussed the differences in our marriages. It really wasn't important to them or us, even though all of our friends were married within their ethnicity. We would have conversations with them a few times, and some questions would arise. One foolish question was, "What was it like being in an interethnic marriage?" Never quite sure how to answer that, I would just say, "Probably the same as being in any type of marriage." How do you answer that? Guessing they were just curious and maybe thought there were some differences. The only difference I can imagine is people treated the same ethnic married couples differently than they treated multi-ethnic couples. We would get strange looks and odd reactions whenever we were out shopping or doing anything as a couple. And still do occasionally. That is where the differences are.

A few times, we would be shopping with the girls when they were very young, and people would say to us, "You people make the cutest babies." What? Yep, that happened many times, and it was hard to understand that type of statement. What possesses a person to make such a statement? And who are "You people"? The gall!

When I was in the Army stationed at Fort Bragg, NC, there was an E5 Sargent who harassed me daily about my marriage. He was Black and from a small town in Arkansas. He would tell me, "Why'd you have to get one of our girls? Can't you get a White girl?" He would also say, "Private Portwine, why did you marry a Black girl? You know it isn't right?" Understanding these questions was difficult because all I saw was a beautiful woman. Not sure whatever happened to him. I am sure God dealt with him regarding his ignorance.

That was something I had to learn. Let God. As someone who likes being in control and tackling things head-on, it was hard for me allowing God to mend, repair, or handle these issues. Although, I have learned to let God overhaul those types of stupidities. It just took me some time. Even today, I want to take the challenges on and deal out my own righteous indignation justice. However, God! That is where I needed to fit in, in God. I have to admit it was extremely hard because I wanted to fix everything. That is what I do, repair, or at least try to repair everything in my realm, whether by debate or by fight. When it came to fight or flight, I always chose the first one. It took God and Felicia to get me to a place of accepting that people are blind; they only see the exterior and never take the time to get to know the interior of a person. Fighting was a childish act, one I committed frequently in high school, thus the weeding out. When we moved back to Arkansas, I had to calm my aggressiveness. Every move had new challenges and required starting over.

Every time we moved into a new house, the neighbors would be standoffish and not speak to us. The funny thing is after they got to know us and saw we were just people, they hated to see us leave the neighborhood and move to another house, another neighborhood, as we had more walls to break down. They had realized Felicia and Ron are just people, good people, and have love for everyone. As I type this, I now know that is where we fit in. I fit in! To show the love of God to everyone and treat them with great respect, the way we want to be treated. Remember, we are all part of the human race, just from different ethnic family backgrounds. I am every day still learning to "Let God."

CHAPTER FIVE

MIXED UP! CHILDREN

FELICIA

Children are a blessing from God. To this union were birthed two amazing and talented daughters. Our girls (young ladies) are four years apart. One has my personality and the other Ron's personality. How many can testify that of their children? See, we are just people. I'm learning, as years are moving on, of some of the struggles they endured growing up. First and foremost, they didn't ask to come into this world. And they most certainly didn't ask for a **Black** mother and **White** father! However, let's talk about how society tries to dictate how we should look, how we should act, how we should talk, etc. All based on the color of our skin.

Knowledge is powerful. Proverbs 4:7 (NKJV) states, "And in all your getting, get understanding." This is key to knowing who our daughters are, understand our bi-ethnic daughters are just that, our daughters. At an early age, we sat them down and tried to explain that they were who they were and didn't have to choose (Black or White). They could be whoever they wanted to be as long as it lined up with the word of God and as long as it was not illegal or immoral. We focused on guiding them to understand and know they were NOT inferior and they did not have to fit into a mold society dictates. Eleanor Roosevelt stated, "No one can make you feel inferior without your consent." (Roosevelt, E., 2020, January 25). Even though we did our best to instill this in them, they still had to face the world themselves. The hardest part was knowing they felt they had to choose which side they wanted to be on. Hear how that sounds? What does this mean, which side? Just what I said, society says you are either Black or White, but why couldn't they be both? Their mother is Black, and their father is White. But unfortunately, to no avail, they had their struggles in deciding who they would be or become, according to what society said they had to be. Why is this so important to society? Maybe you are guilty of this. Not because you want to be, but because you were raised to classify people, putting them in small, defined boxes. This is something the girls had to face daily, how people boxed them in—even friends.

One set of friends would say they were too White while the other set said they were too Black. I mean, really!! Talk about peer pressure to the nth degree. Those were just a few things they had to deal with, friends and their preconceived ideas. The dating was just as bad. Anytime I would say, "Oh yeah, the girls are dating," the first question was, "Are they Black or White?" It was as if people/family (mostly family) wanted to see if they were following in my footsteps. Just because their parents were interethnic, I guess they wanted to see if our daughters would also have interethnic relationships, erring on the White side like their mother. Crazy, crazy, and crazy!!!!

Like Ron and I, they too have a destiny, and it's not left up to any of us to dictate what that ensues, even though Ron and I would like to play a part in that (as parents). You know the part of choosing that someone who would love them for them. It's not what we want but what God has for them. With the pressures of choosing which side they were on, we also had to figure the hair thing out. Let's talk or not talk about the hair issues. This could be an exhaustive topic, to say the least.

OMG!!! I was raised believing Vaseline could fix anything. WRONG! As I laugh. I mean, product after product, having bi-babies, you just don't know what hair type they will have. One had kinky hair and needed certain kinds of hair treatment, and the other one had straight hair (somewhat) and needed a whole set of other hair treatments. This also led to some of the identity problems they faced constantly. People would see their hair and accuse them of trying to be Black or White based on straight or kinky. Again something they had no control over.

Although this came with the territory, unfortunately, the madness was real, but they/we survived. I think I felt the pain more intense than their dad. Why you ask, because I'm a Black woman. Don't misunderstand; Ron was /is very involved and hands-on in their lives. However, I had to be more real or open in a sense because I was already familiar with the struggle of racism and felt they would understand why I/we felt the need to prepare them for the real world. First, they are bi-ethnic, which means BLACK, and second, they were women. It was as if the odds were stacked against them from the beginning despite their ethnicity (Bi). Get the picture? I've never shied away from being real with them. Society says if there is one ounce of Black, then you are Black. This is ignorance gone to seed and is rooted in stupidity. We did our best to prepare them for the world they would live in.

We always told them they had to study and work harder than the average person. I'm sure the Black community can attest to these words. It sounds horrible saying it out loud, but it was/is real. On the other hand, one of the biggest things Ron and I instilled in them the most was education. Knowledge is powerful. Yes, we know education doesn't change racism, but it helps. We would tell them no one could take their education or knowledge from them. Defy the odds, we would say. So with that being said, our oldest went on to earn her Masters in Fine Arts, and our youngest daughter served in the United States Navy (thanks for your service). She was accepted into the Naval Academy before a medical condition got in the way of her future plans of retiring as an Officer. She proceeded on in obtaining an Associate of Science in Culinary, Associates of General Studies with an emphasis in Computer

Science, has earned her Real Estate License, owns a Vegan Business, is married, and most importantly, a mother to our granddaughter.

See, your ending is all in God's hands, not societies. We are very proud of the young women they have become despite their painful beginnings. Just because their beginnings were rough doesn't mean that has to be the end of their story. As Jeremiah 29:11 (NKJV) states, "For I know the thoughts that I think toward you, says the Lord, thoughts of peace and not of evil, to give you a future hope." God knows the plans He has for each of us. Allow His plans to work!

RONALD

The two greatest gifts Felicia gave me besides her LOVE are our daughters. These two beautiful girls were tested daily when they got into school. It didn't matter what grade they were in, as they were classified every step of the way. By children, teachers, and any adult they may have come in contact with. It was painful for me to witness this, knowing they were just girls that I loved and only wanted the best for them. Their school years were tough, and they often had to choose. This wasn't fair for them, and it should never be that way! I knew society would classify them into a certain ethnic group. Which really didn't matter; I just wanted them to choose who they knew they were within themselves. Why does society classify multi-ethnic people as one or the other? What is wrong with just letting them be? Struggling every day with this question, my heart would be wounded, disdained by this senseless idea of hatred because of skin color. I am unable to comprehend this and pray I never do! As their father seeing this prejudice and disparity all over again made me livid.

WHY? I still just do not understand. This is why I would convey to them; be who God says they are and treat everyone the same regardless of how they act or react towards you. Their actions towards you show who they really are. Be mindful of them and be cordial, just don't let them get under your skin and grow aggrieved or wish to be different. Stand your ground and never lash out when treated wrongly. Be unapologetically you! Those children/people just don't understand yet. Always telling my girls to be themselves and not try to fit in anywhere; let it be natural, and true friends will reveal themselves over time.

Both had friends from various ethnic backgrounds, and that was okay. If they chose to err on the White side, okay; if they chose to err on the Black side, okay. To me, it was that simple. But it wasn't for them. WHY? This could be a question that never gets answered because of ignorance; however, I pray that someday the difference in skin tone will be history and a futile subject.

Being of multi-ethnicity, there are some huge hurdles to cross. No matter what we told them, they would have to stand on their own and make quality decisions that would dictate their life's journeys. It was very hard for me to learn of the many times they were called names or so-called friends would speak destructively about them. I remember when our oldest came home one time and said they called her banana – not a term of endearment but one of derision. I explained to her these were not true friends and to let them fade out of her life and move on. That is tough to do in high school, especially when this is a time of upheaval and finding one's path and learning who you are. Our youngest had friends from all ethnicities and was somewhat more in your face than the oldest. She would deal with the prejudices head-on. She would nip it in the bud and stop the friendship. She was more like me, outspoken, and basically didn't care what people thought about her as much as the oldest. Growing up during this time was a progressive journey, and they became the best parts of Felicia and I within time.

As they got older and moved on past high school, they came into their own and became strong young ladies. They faced the crazy world head-on and did not allow people to sway them away from how Felicia and I raised them. I know it was not easy, but they came through like victors and not victims. Ensuring I was there to support them in whatever decision they made was the key to giving them solid structural support. Our oldest moved on and worked her way through college and earned her Master's, something no one in my family had ever done.

She ventured into an academic arena that was predominantly White - Theater. With that degree, I have seen her take on so many challenges as she utilized her degrees to the fullest when dealing with all ethnicities. Theater gave her tremendous insights into people and how to recognize phony. Something many people never learn at any age. When our youngest finished high school, she decided to go another route.

It was a proud day for Felicia and me when she was sworn in as a sailor. She enlisted in the NAVY and journeyed out into the world. She had to break through walls when she got out there, and I am so very proud of her for standing her ground. She excelled at the tasks set before her and impacted those she came in contact with. That is something both of them have done. They have changed many people's perceptions of multi-ethnic preconceived ideas concerning anyone of off-color.

The individuals they have become have been something Felicia and I are very proud of. They continue to show us they have not allowed past acquaintances or circumstances to dictate who they are. Even though school was tough, they made sure they followed the same guidance as I did based on my mother's teachings. Reminding them, "Yes, you are different; however, be you and never judge people by the color of their skin and treat everyone equally and with dignity, and most importantly with the love of God." My goal was to give them sound advice to live a life that shows people they are different and yet the same. They will never allow people's actions towards them or people's preconceived ideas about them to dictate how they treat others. Even in 2022, people still hold on to these issues. This is a bitter pill to swallow, especially when people are harsh, rude, and uncaring. Felicia and I still remind our girls to be who they are and show the love of God to everyone no matter what.

Seeing them continue to grow, I now realize they will be okay. They have made some good and bad choices. Who hasn't? Seeing them now as overcoming the prejudices of their younger years has given me a sense of having given them a strong foundation, and we taught them correctly. I know they still meet people in life, who see them as a certain ethnic group, and you know what, it doesn't matter. That's those people's problem. They can shrug off the ignorance, indifference, and irrelevant preconceived ideas and keep moving without any residual impacts. My girls are strong, and I am 100% sure they are not allowing the world to push them one way or the other. Choices, we all have them.

People must get past the skin color issue and see people as people of the human race. Yes, we are different, and yes, I am not ignorant to think otherwise. My mother was right, "Never judge a person by the color of their skin." Proverbs 22:6 (NKJV) states, "Train up a child in the way he (she) should go, and when he (she) is old, he (she) will not depart from it." My girls are following a path that has had some turns along the way; however, they are true to never judging people based on anything other than their character and then loving them. As you read these words, I pray there is an urgency within you to let go of those hate-filled learnings and accept that GOD created us all equal in His image (Genesis 1:26-27, 5:1-2). It can be hard to let go of lifelong learnings. Nonetheless, it is doable. Remember, people are just people; they come from different ethnic backgrounds. Let these words resonate within you as you raise your children. Please teach them every one is never to be judged or placed in a category of ridicule or contempt because of the color of their skin.

I want to end this chapter with a funny side note. Once the girls got older, I would tell them I married a Black woman because I wanted my children to have a year-round tan. Yep, I said it, just for grins. They would always take it with a grain of salt, knowing I was having fun.

CHAPTER SIX

HAPPILY EVER AFTER FOREVER I DO

FELICIA

"Forever I Do" (Lou Rawls, January 1984). That was **our** wedding song. It feels like yesterday, although it's been over thirty-five-plus years. We were just kids. He was twenty-one, and I was twenty. It's funny how that felt okay, but the thought of our girls marrying that young is unthinkable. We are growing old together. It has been a long and sometimes hard journey, but as I used to hear the older folks say, "I wouldn't take anything for my journey." A marriage of love, harmony, and acceptance is not grounded in passion; it is entrenched in worship. God alone ordains a marriage. I am so thankful God ordained and predestined Ron for me and me for him. Despite **our** tough and insane beginnings, God has remained faithful to **our** union. I can remember walking down the aisle thinking, this is it, and I'm really getting married. **I'z married now**!! LOL. Okay, let's get back on track.

Our wedding colors were Burgundy and Ivory; remember, it was 1986. Ron's mom made my wedding dress and the bridesmaid's dresses. The morning of the wedding, we decided to take a drive and talk; of course, Ron wanted to make sure this was what I wanted to do as he was very sure this was what he wanted. Of course, I assured him this was what I wanted also. I have no regrets, and I would do it again without hesitation. Ron has stood by his vows when we were up and when we were down, laughing and crying, in sickness and health, as I, too, have stood by mine. We have been in awe of God's divine plan for **our** lives. Again despite the rough beginnings, God has shown us His favor in and out of season.

As stated in an earlier chapter, after about eleven years of marriage, my dad had a change of heart (I guess he thought; well, he (Ron) isn't leaving, so I might as well join them). My mother soon realized that Ron wasn't so bad after all. Talk about a turnaround. Even though they felt the way they did, we never disrespected them and always continued **our** walk with God and allowed Him to change their hearts. For the first six years of our marriage, I was a stay-at-home wife and mother, as the first baby came three months after our one-year anniversary. What seemed like a struggle at first really was the best beginning of what has lasted over thirty-five-plus years. Side note: Advice to a young wife and mother; if you can afford to stay home with your babies and you and your spouse agree, stay. You won't regret it.

Family should always be a priority. I'm thankful for the man God predestined for me. He has been more than I could have ever imagined. Ron has loved unconditionally and has worked hard at being the man, husband, and father for his family. There was never a time I had to question his love for me and the girls. He has proven through the years that we were/are his priority. Ron has never swayed from his duties as head of our household. As Christ laid down His life for us, Ron has laid his life down for this family. Because of his tenacity and perseverance, Ron has over thirty years of knowledge in the machine tool industry, served in the U.S. Army (thank you for your service); Ron has also earned two Associates, a Bachelor's, and his Master's Degree. He currently works for the world's largest round cutting tool manufacturer globally. It's not Black, and it's not White. Ron has proven to be a man of God at all costs.

Allow God to open your minds and hearts to what He wants to do in your life. An interethnic relationship is not for everyone, only those

God preordains. We must be willing not to judge a person based on the color of their skin but by the content of their character/heart. Dr. Martin Luther King Jr. stated, "I have a dream, a dream one day this nation will rise up and live up to its creed. We hold these truths to be self-evident: that all men are created equal." (King Jr., M. L., November 5, 2021)

We are all God's children, red, yellow, black, and white. We are precious in His sight. I also remember walking down the aisle thinking, Wow, he really loves me, and I'm going to be his wife. No regrets and no apologies. Reflecting on our wedding song "Forever I Do" by Lou Rawls. I endlessly will hold onto Ron and give my very life for him devotionally and will hold his hand into the future because when I said I DO, it wasn't just words; it was a forever commitment before God. God alone ordained this marriage before time ever existed. According to dictionary.com, forever is an "endless or seemingly endless period of time; without ever ending; eternally." April 5, 1986, the beginning of a forever marriage.

RONALD

I had never heard that song until Felicia told me about it. We went to a local music store and purchased the cassette tape. After listening to it the first time, I knew it was right. It was perfect because that is what I was committed to, "FOREVER, I DO"! My experience/knowledge of marriages had been, to say the least, poor. Happily ever after's were not witnessed within my immediate family. The only thing I was sure of was my resolve to do everything in my capabilities to take care of Felicia and make our lives better than what we both witnessed growing up. My focus and determination were to be the best husband I could be. Although there were no good examples in my family, I had to make a conscious decision to be/do better. Not knowing what a husband should look like or be like, I solely relied on God. All I had was what God imparted in me and what the Word revealed along the way.

My desire to be a good husband drove me to do what had to be done to take care of Felicia and our girls. I would work two or three jobs to ensure all needs were met. I would also work on cars in the evenings and on weekends to make extra for when they needed something outside the norm. I would push myself to make sure my girls knew what a dedicated husband and father would do for his family and what he looked like. The overwhelming push for this made me reflect on what **not** to do as a husband. What I witnessed growing up was nowhere close to what I now know to be what God says about marriage. This has been my determination throughout **our** marriage; from day one, I wanted to do what was right and make sure others saw my faithfulness as a husband. When the girls came along, I had another purpose, being a father. Giving them the best example of a good husband and father was a priority. These were all the more reasons I was driven to be the best I could conceivably be. Not knowing the future or what it held, the only thing I was sure of was that I was going to set the tone for my family. As the wedding day quickly approached, I knew I was stepping into the most important trek of my life.

Yes, we went for a drive on the day of the wedding, and I had several questions to ask Felicia. At this point, I was 1000% sure this was what I was supposed to do and wanted to do. The thing was, I wanted to make sure Felicia was certain. Her happiness was more important to me than she knew. I did not want her to feel any pressure going into this marriage and needed her confirmation. As we drove around, I remembered what some of my so-called friends, who are no longer in my life, said to me. I now know they didn't mean any harm; they were just making statements based on what they saw growing up. Unfortunately, many of them also had poor family examples, which dictated their thought processes and even their actions in their own marriages.

Two of them, in particular, said, "Portwine, you probably won't make one year of marriage. Little did they know, as I now know, this was entirely part of God's divine plan. After seeing my mother's failed marriages, I knew that was not what I wanted. After one year passed, I had heard some say two years would be it, and then at five years, I heard it again. "Ron and Felicia will not make ten years." Well, some of those same people have been married and divorced multiple times, while Felicia and I have weathered every trial, tribulation, and tempest that has come against us. We were resolute to stay together no matter what. While Felicia and I made sure God was in the midst from the very beginning. Yes, we had some difficulties along the way and made some wrong decisions but never concerning our faithfulness to our marriage and each other. Overwhelmingly we always stood by each other's side and purposed to stick this thing out for good or bad, richer or poorer, in sickness or in health, we would grow old together as God intended. Throwing in the towel was not an option. Knowing this was the woman I was to be with from age thirteen assured me, without a doubt, we could do this.

God placed this woman in my heart, and no matter what may have come against us, I was not letting her go. She has been the overwhelming reason I push myself to be a better man, husband, and father. I have endeavored to be a great provider for her and our girls, no matter the cost. My desire from the beginning has always been to take care of Felicia and give her a better life than what she was accustomed to. I may not have had good husband or fatherly examples; however, I did have an example of how to work and provide.

My stepfather at the time was a workaholic. After long nights of helping him, I would soon realize he may not have been the husband example I needed; however, he was the example of a working man who provided. For these thirty-five-plus years, this has been me (Ron), and I will continue to be me for another thirty-five-plus years, I pray! To be a husband willing to work, sacrifice, do what it takes to provide, stand as a man of God, do my best to echo His word in everything I set my hands to. I have never compromised this belief and never will.

One day early on in the marriage, about our third year, God spoke to me and said, "Ron, you and Felicia will be together well into your eighties." I have spoken that to Felicia more times than I can count and will continue to stand on His promise. God predestined us as a married couple. Emphasizing **to each other!** I have prayed and asked God for us to live long and have a quality God-fearing life. Believing, without doubt, God will give me more time on earth with this beautiful woman, as he did for Hezekiah in Ezekiel 38, adding fifteen years to his life. I believe God will add more to our lives. Happiness is relevant, and I know God wants us to live happily ever after. I strived to put God first in our marriage and have always looked to Him for answers and directions. My overwhelming desire has constantly been to take care of Felicia. I have been accused of being wrapped around her finger. The truth is, I do for Felicia because she does for me. There are no strings. Just love! Besides, I am good with being wrapped around her finger!!

In the summer of 1999, I was on a fast for several days, asking God for direction in ministry, life, work, finances, etc. When I came to the end of the fast, I clearly heard God say to me, "Ron, be a man, a husband, and a father, and I (God) will take care of everything else." That has been my stance since then. I must do my part and let God handle the things out of my control. That is very difficult for me; as I stated earlier in the book, I am a fixer. However, when I made that my refrain and got out of God's way, miracles on every side became the norm in life.

As we now draw near the end of this book, you may ask, "Are you happy, Ron?" I can say with no hesitations, "YES, I AM HAPPY." I am happy for what God has given me in a wife, happy for my two beautiful daughters and granddaughter, and happy to be in a Godly marriage that goes well beyond skin color and preconceived opinions. Happy Felicia said yes, after the "Are you serious?" My spirit, body, heart, and soul, everything I am or will ever be, is wrapped up in this happily ever after. Forever I Do! These are more than just three words!!! I read a quote somewhere that kind of sums it up. "She focused on God; he did the same. God gave them each other." (Author unknown)

CHAPTER 7

LAST WORDS
THE CHURCH

FELICIA

The Church. Yep, the Church!! Where do we begin? "Any time your ethnic heritage is more important than your connection to Jesus, you are in trouble. That only leads to arrogance, pride, and division. First and foremost, we are all of God's family-the body of Christ." (Pastor Rod Loy). We must conclude that God alone has the last word. I grew up in the church, so this was a norm for me; however, I really don't recall ever seeing other ethnicities worshiping with us. Why is that? I don't have an answer. After Ron and I were married, we started attending the church he was baptized in at age eleven. It was actually an all-Black congregation. However, because church wasn't something taught or pushed in his home, he soon strayed away. On the other hand, I myself had strayed when I left home also, but how many know once the seed has been planted, it will come forth. Proverbs 22:6 states, "Train up a child in the way he should go: and when he is old, he will not depart from it." (NKJV).

With that being said, Ron and I wanted to make sure God was at the center of **our** marriage, so we joined the church where he was baptized. The Pastor remembered baptizing him and made sure that event was a part of his sermons regularly. Lol. And of course, how could he forget? I mean, Ron was the only, well, you know. We rededicated our lives back to Christ, and we both soon got involved in the church by first joining the choir. Back then, you didn't have to audition. They just took your word as to whether you were a soprano, alto, tenor, or bass. Ron also became an Usher. So we were heavily involved in the church early on in our marriage. Our Pastor was a great man of God and was well known in the community. He would frequently get asked to preach at other churches for their afternoon programs. We made a point to support and follow him to the various churches. By the way, for some reason, the Mother Board really took a liking to Ron. That's funny!! Anyway, it didn't matter whether we were having service at our church or visiting another church, our Pastor made it a point to have Ron stand and announce that he was his White member. Funny right!!! As if people hadn't noticed.

This went on for quite some time, and finally, I told Ron if he stood up one more time, I would walk out of the church. He and I still laugh about that to this day. We know there was no harm intended, but why???? Then there were those times when we were treated very ugly (in the church). Again, why??? The church is a place of refuge and a place that teaches about God's love, the first commandment.

I remember when our oldest was born, and I had returned to church. I was sitting in the front row, and it was offering time. Those who grew up in a Black church will remember that during the offering, you had to walk around to the front to put your offering in the bucket. So as this was taking place, I recall Pastor telling everyone to walk by and look at the baby. What I thought to myself was, "Are you kidding me?" But again, I know no pun was intended. However, I'm just saying was all that necessary just because Ron was the only White member at that time.

Remembering one Sunday night, we had service, and we had a guest minister that was to speak, I kid you not when I say this minister got up and started preaching and saying Black and White was not to marry and how this was a disgrace to God. This was very hurtful, especially coming from the pulpit. So you're telling me that God changed his sermon to preach and make a point to let the church know (according to him) being married outside your ethnicity was a sin. Or was this his own agenda when he saw Ron? We expect the world/society to shun or have preconceived ideas and beliefs regarding multi-ethnic marriages, but not the church. Jesus died for all, red, yellow, black, and white. Again this was very hurtful; however, because Ron and I knew who we were in Christ, we actually felt sorry for that minister. Even then, we knew that wasn't right. There was never a point in our marriage that we questioned whether or not we were outside the will of God. Thank God our Pastor apologized and never invited that minister again.

As the years went on and we allowed God to order our footsteps, each time we moved and became new members at a church (and no, we were not church hoppers), it has always felt as if we were breaking down barriers. We were tearing down stereotypes in a sense. Some were more welcoming than others, and yes, I'm still referring to the church. I know times have changed, and I'm very thankful that the church is opening up more in this area. Churches have most definitely come a long way. We are finally moving in the direction of coming together as one body and in one accord. This is to fulfill and execute the same agenda, which is to worship the Most High and go out into a dying world, letting them know Jesus died and rose for them.

Quite frankly, we are the church, not the building. We are learning to embrace the fact that, yes, we are different but yet the same in the eyes of the Lord. I believe the church has come to a conclusion on the matter, there is no Black heaven, and there is no White heaven. Just a Heaven. I know we still have a long way to go, and my prayer is we get this thing right before it's too late. Lives need to be saved, and we are the only Jesus many people in this world will ever see. I commission the church to step back and make the real thing the real thing. Christ is coming back for a church without a spot or wrinkle. Not a Black church, not a White church, but for His church. So again, let us not judge according to a person's skin tone but according to how God sees them and who God says they/we are. And as far as **our** marriage is concerned, I'm a firm believer that God Himself predestined and ordained for this union to be. Unapologetically. And if He ordained it, who are we/society to say otherwise. Who you choose to be your husband or wife (as ordained of God) impacts every aspect of your life. Mental health, physical health, peace of mind, happiness, and love within, getting through tragedies, success, raising your children, and so much more dictate that **you must choose wisely!**

RONALD

Where do I begin? The only thing capable of transforming people is the force of Love. The church has given me some fantastic memories, all of them unique. As Felicia stated, we would follow our Pastor as he would travel and minister at other churches around Arkansas. He would often make it a point to introduce me as his White member. This was always funny to me and made me feel as though I was his trophy member. Understand this was over thirty years ago in Arkansas. I never thought he was doing this out of ill will, only to crow. Often when visiting small-town churches, the members would look at me oddly. Some were a bit standoffish, and I am sure were wondering why is he here. Pastor would often have me sit on the front pew in many of the churches as to say he (Ron) is just as we are, human. Even though I was the only White member at the time, he welcomed me with open arms, and I will cherish that for the rest of my life.

One time, in particular, I was sitting in the front, and a young boy, about seven or eight years old, was sitting next to me. He would look at me and then at the mural on the wall behind the pulpit. The mural was a painting of Jesus with open arms standing in a river. Many of the churches we visited had a mural of Jesus in some fashion behind the pulpit. This youngster looked at me and looked back at the mural. He did this several times, then looked at me, tapped me on the arm, and asked me a question. I knew where he was going because, at the time, I had a full beard and wore my hair a little longer. This gave him a thought which could only be addressed by asking me a question. After him tapping me on the arm, I said, "Yes, young man? How may I help you?" He looked up at me and asked, "Are you Jesus?" It took all I had not to laugh. I said to him, "No, I am not Jesus." He appeared to be dismayed while I was still laughing within. I guess he was thinking what other White man would be in "**his**" church if not Jesus. He stayed next to me through the whole service and would look at me and back at the mural. I sometimes wonder where that young man is today and does he reflect on that event.

These events sometimes would solidify my thoughts about Black churches. Not in a bad way. It was just obvious they probably did not ask many White people to come to their church, or they did ask, and they chose not to visit. I'm only speaking of the Black church because that is what I was accustomed to. I'm sure it was just as obvious in the White churches as well. Probably a bit more. Either way, my experiences in the Black churches ran the full gambit.

One of the issues that got to me the most, and still does to this day, is when I would speak to someone in the church, and they would ignore me, refuse to make eye contact, or just wouldn't shake my hand. Some would turn their heads and walk around me as if trying to avoid me. It was as if they were saying I was not welcome and should not be there. This often happened at the larger Black churches where I had become a member, churches where the pastors would minister at times concerning all ethnic groups and how all should come together as one church. It was painful when this happened because I have never done anything to reflect something other than the love of God. I would vent my frustration with Felicia, and she would allow me to speak and then remind me, it's not about us and say again that maybe we were there to break barriers.

But why me, Lord? Why Felicia and I? It runs through me like a knife, and I want to go back and give them some choice words to let them know they were WRONG!! Again Felicia would say, is it really worth it? In my mind, YES! Rest assured, I never did. I have accepted this and believe we are to do just that, break down barriers, prejudices, and ideologies! Showing them, we are just people. JUST PEOPLE! Is that so hard to understand? I suppose I always knew this; my flesh just gets tired. Sometimes I want to put Jesus on a shelf and, well, you know.

I have heard it said that what irritates you the most is what you are called to. I despise prejudice, racism, bigotry, and any form of discrimination. My prayer is for God to give me the grace to be a symbol of love for people, to witness, and always to remember people are just people, staying focused on my mother's teachings. As you finish this book, I pray that you will also know people are just people. Everyone is part of the human race, just different ethnicities and backgrounds. Show love to everyone as Christ did; it is life-changing for them and you. Love is the most important thing; Love is what binds everything together. 1 Peter 4:8 (NKJV) states, "And above all things have fervent love for one another, for *"love will cover a multitude of sins."* Again this has been **our** journey.

"We must learn to live together as brothers or perish together as fools." – (Dr. Martin Luther King Jr., Goodreads)

It was June 12, 1967, when the U.S. Supreme Court ruled it was illegal to declare prohibitions about interracial marriage and thus was unconstitutional in the U.S.

According to an article on npr.com, Chief Justice Earl Warren wrote the opinion for the court; he wrote that marriage is a basic civil right and to deny this right on the basis of color is "directly subversive of the principle of equality at the heart of the Fourteenth Amendment" and seizes all citizens "liberty without due process of law." (Grigsby Bates, K., 2021, June 12). June 12 is loving day - when interracial marriage finally became legal in the U.S.

Always remember God's best is yours.
– The Portwines

REFERENCES

Angelou, M. (2013, June 24). "When you know better, do better." Lifehacker. Retrieved October 13, 2021, from https://lifehacker.com/when-you-know-better-do-better-565500764.

Angelou, M. (n.d.). A quote by Maya Angelou. Goodreads. Retrieved November 5, 2021, from https://www.goodreads.com/quotes/335-when-someone-shows-you-who-they-are-believe-them-the.

"Forever." Retrieved March 20, 222 from https://www.dictionary.com/browse/forever.

Grigsby Bates, K. (2021, June 12). U.S. NPR. Retrieved March 22, 2022, from https://www.npr.org/2021/06/12/1005848169/loving-day-interracial-marriage-legal-origin

King Jr., M. L., (2015, April 11). "Injustice anywhere is a threat to justice everywhere." US History Scene. Retrieved November 5, 2021, from https://ushistoryscene.com/article/birmingham-manifesto.

King Jr., M. L. (n.d.). A quote by Martin Luther King Jr. Goodreads. Retrieved December 1, 2021 from https://www.goodreads.com/quotes/23673-we-must-live-together-as-brothers-or-perish-together-as.

King Jr., M. L. (n.d.). Martin Luther King Jr. I have a dream speech - American rhetoric. Retrieved November 5, 2021, from https://www.americanrhetoric.com/speeches/mlkihaveadream.htm.

Roosevelt, E. (2020, January 25). "Thoughts on Life and Love." Retrieved September 11, 2021, from https://www.thoughtsonlifeandlove.com/no-one-can-make-you-feel-inferior-without-your-consent/27878.

www.ingramcontent.com/pod-product-compliance
Lightning Source LLC
Chambersburg PA
CBHW062141100526
44589CB00014B/1650